You matter ♡
xoxoxo –

A Girl With A ^Pink Cape

Written by Amy Logan

Illustrated by Rich Green

Full Heart Publishing

A portion of the profits from each book sold goes to local charities.

Published by

Full Heart Publishing, Full Heart, LLC

Printed in USA

Title fonts courtesy of *Fontscafe.com*, Copyright 2012

Amy's headshot courtesy of *Moments by A*. Copyright 2013

First Edition, First Print

ISBN-13: 978-0-9890465-3-4

GotYourCape.com

For my sister, Michelle

In December of 2004, two days before Christmas, my sister, Michelle, was diagnosed with breast cancer. She beat it. In 2012, it returned. It returned as *metastatic* breast cancer. *"Metastasis refers to the spread of cancer to different parts of the body and vital organs, typically the bones, liver, lungs and brain."*

And that's *exactly* what it did.

She endured another 15 months of chemotherapy. That is, until her body quietly said, *"enough."*

On Sunday, April 13, 2014, around 7:00 in the morning, my sister passed away.

Life is precious. It moves so fast, only you don't realize it when you're in the trenches.

On April 2nd, when my sister went into the hospital because of a fever and not feeling well, we never thought in a million years *"this"* would be the time that she didn't come home. Life sped up at that moment. By a lot. Times a million. And the worst part of it? We can never get that, *or any,* time back. Once it's gone, that's it. And there is never, ever, *ever* enough time.

This book is for you, Michelle, and for all those who are battling something, *anything*. This book is for those who are reading this, right at this moment. And, it's for those who make kindness a daily thing like lending a hand, or an ear, or an hour to someone who needs it. And sometimes, you never really know *who* needs it, you just do it because *that's* who you are. Truth is... *You* matter. *Your kindnesses* matter. *Everything you do,* matters.

May we all learn to live like that – like heroes – making the most out of our precious time here on earth. May we love on people more, including ourselves; may we truly believe that we have purpose here; and may we all completely and wholeheartedly realize that no matter what, no matter the differences, no matter the circumstances, we *all* matter. Time moves too fast to live any other way.

Michelle, I love you and I miss you every day. I will always cherish the words you put on my heart shortly after you passed to calm my aching soul. From the Heavens, you said to me:

> *"I know you're sad.*
> *Grieve if you must,*
> *But I'm okay.*
> *In God keep trust.*
> *I'll see you soon;*
> *Don't count the days,*
> *Just live and love*
> *And sing His praise."*
> - April 2014

You, are my hero. And this is for you.
xoxoxo

Sometimes we think heroes work really long hours,
have really big muscles and really strong powers.
And if we don't have that "Why bother!" we say.
"I'm not all that super! I'm not! Go away!"
But, this super story may make you think twice.
Sometimes our biggest power is just to be nice.

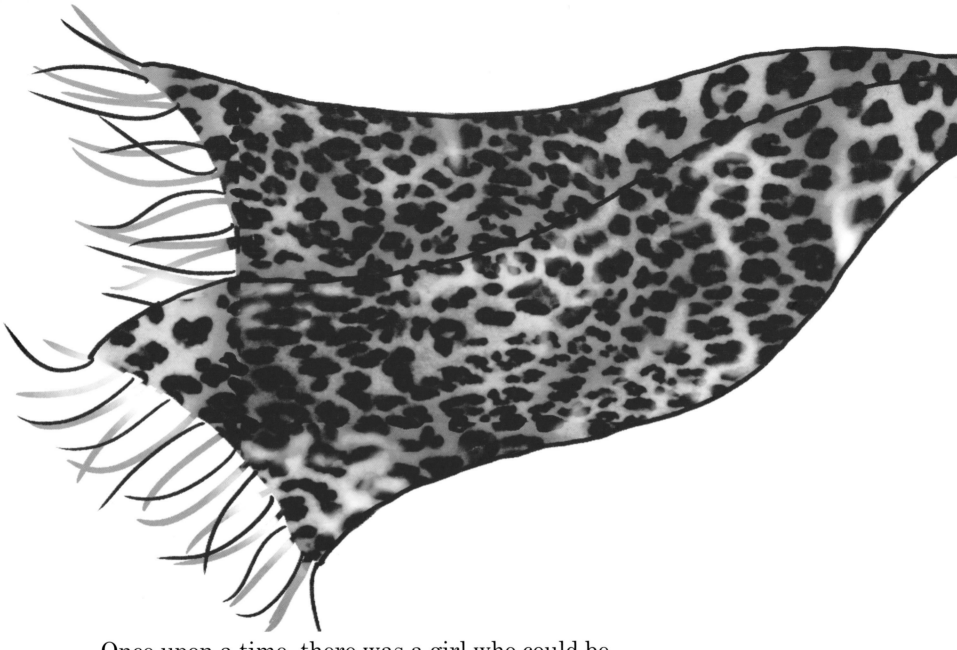

Once upon a time, there was a girl who could be
a friend or a neighbor, or you, even me.
She loved to wear capes and she loved to pretend...
and since time is so precious, let's get on with it then.

The day started just like the others before.
With brushed hair and teeth, she was ready for more.

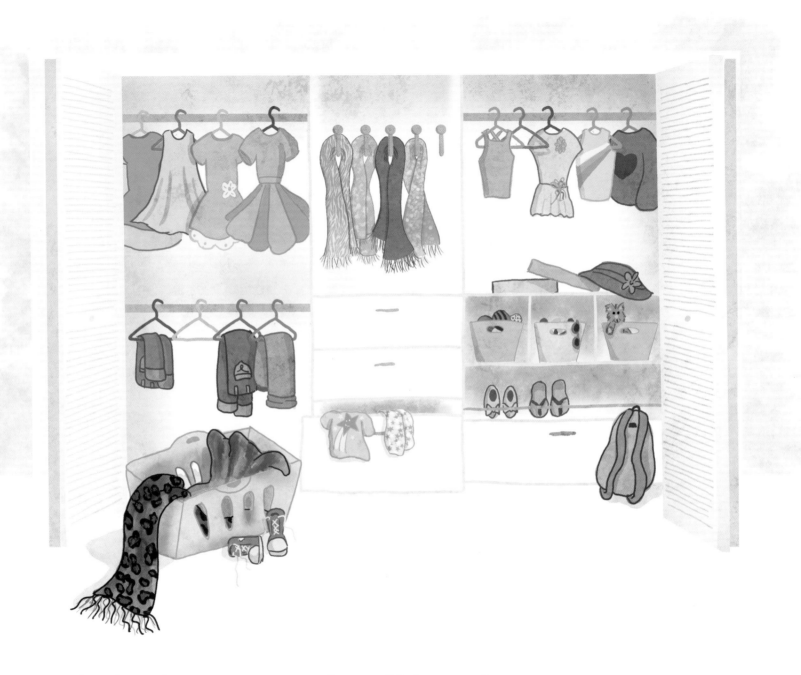

She ran back to her room to get herself dressed.
Whatever she'd play, she should look her best!

Excited! Delighted! And ready to play!
"Yes, THIS is the one I will put on today!
I'll tie it like this! Down my back it will drape!"

"Tadaa! I am super! And here is my cape!"

A girl with a cape saw her friends were out playing.
She wanted to play too, that went without saying.

She ran to ask mom, but saw mom feeling bad.
"Mom, why are you crying? Why are you sad?"

Mom said,
"I just got a call from my friend who's a nurse.
Our neighbor who's sick? She's just gotten worse.
My heart is so heavy. I don't mean to cry
but sit down and let's talk, and I'll explain why."

Mom said that the neighbor stayed mostly in bed,
and she wore her own "cape" on the top of her head.
And even though today was a beautiful day,
Mom asked her daughter if later she'd play
because right now her mom needed her a bit more,
and so did the neighbor who lived right next door.

"But what do I tell her? And what do I say"

"You just go be super, like you are everyday."

A girl with a cape, she thought for a minute...
And THEN an idea, so time to begin it.

She took out her crayons
and made a card.
She helped baked some cookies which wasn't so hard.
She took out a plate
and wrapped it up tight.
A bow on the top, that looks just right.
With a card and her cookies and scarf that she wore,

to the neighbor's she went...
and she knocked on the door.

"I brought you a treat," our super girl said.
"They're easy to eat while you're lying in bed.

My cape means I'm super. My mom told me so,
and you wear one too, which I already know.
So together I thought that good friends we would make
and I'd help you be super and give you a break.

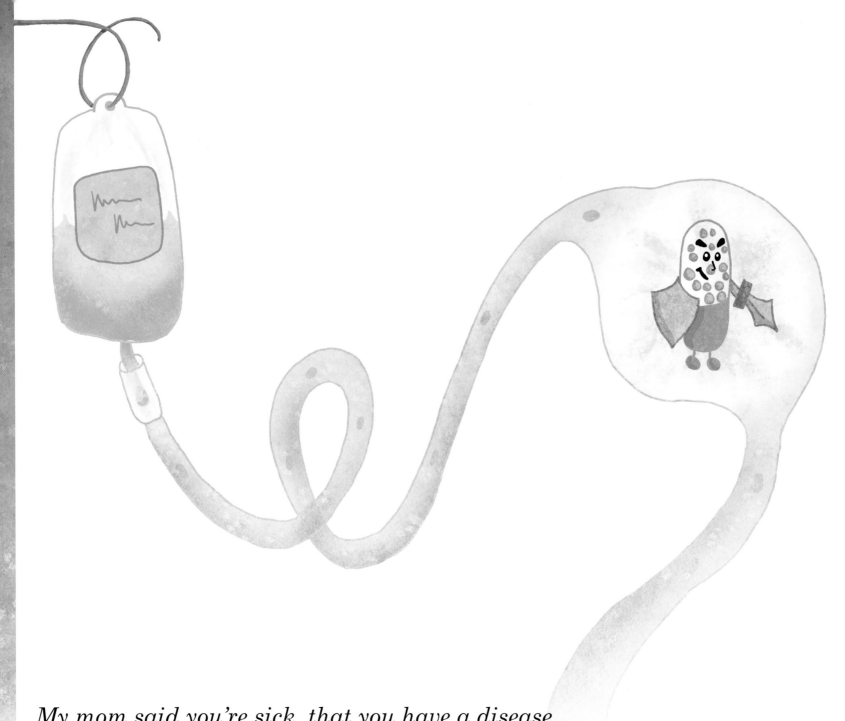

My mom said you're sick, that you have a disease,
And you fight it with medicine that goes through IVs.

She says you're a hero for so many others;
that you fight with courage
for daughters and mothers
and women all over, and even some men,
so I thought that you might need
a break now and then.

The neighbor paused...

"I've never felt super,"
she quietly said.
"I hardly feel super
while lying in bed,
or even at all,"
she then wiped her eyes.
"But now here YOU are.
This is quite a surprise.
Please, won't you come in?
Let's pull up a chair.
I really must say,
I'm so glad that you're here."

They sat at the table enjoying the snack.
They both told some jokes
and they laughed and they laughed.

(...and they *laughed*!)

They played some games.
They watched TV.
They talked and laughed 'til after 3.
They ate more cookies, laughed some more...

...and time flew by. It was now past four.

The neighbor looked down,
and the girl asked, *"What is it?"*

The neighbor said,
"I'm getting very tired,
but so glad for your visit.
As you can imagine, I don't get many guests
so today was a treat, but now I must rest."

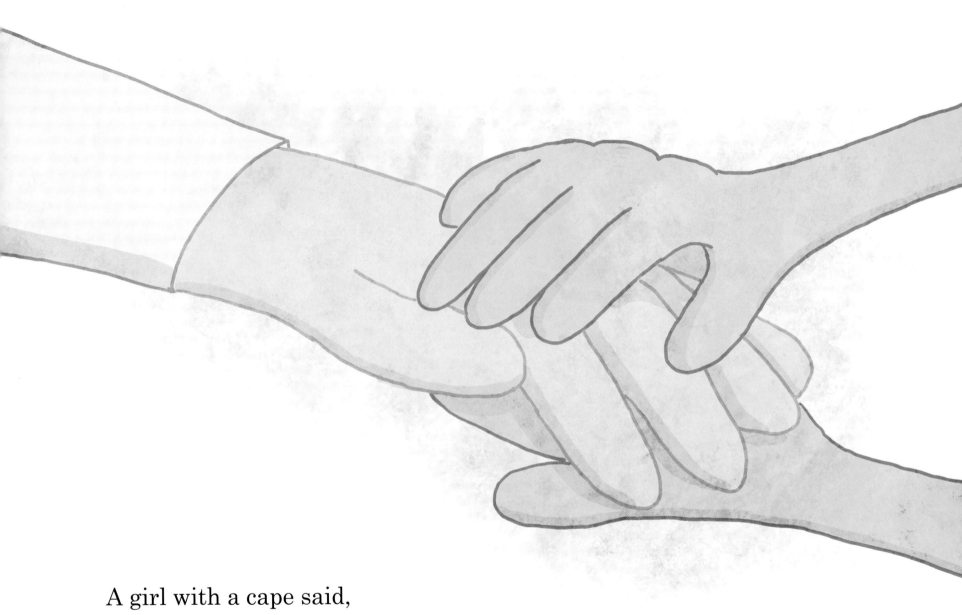

A girl with a cape said,
"*OOH!! I almost forgot.*
It's very important and means a whole lot.
I just need to tell you before I go home,
that you are MY hero, and you're not alone."

The neighbor opened her arms & with all her might,
she hugged a girl with a cape so tight
and said,
"*Sweetie, YOU are the hero. The things that you do:*
The courage, the kindness, the visit, it's YOU.
Sure, I am sick, and some days it's hard,
but you made it better with your cookies and card.
You made me feel special, like I really mattered.
You helped mend my spirit, which feels so shattered.
You've given me hope on a day like today,
for that I am thankful that you came my way."

And right at that moment, unlike any other,
They took of their capes and exchanged with each other.
They smiled. They hugged. The each gave a wink…

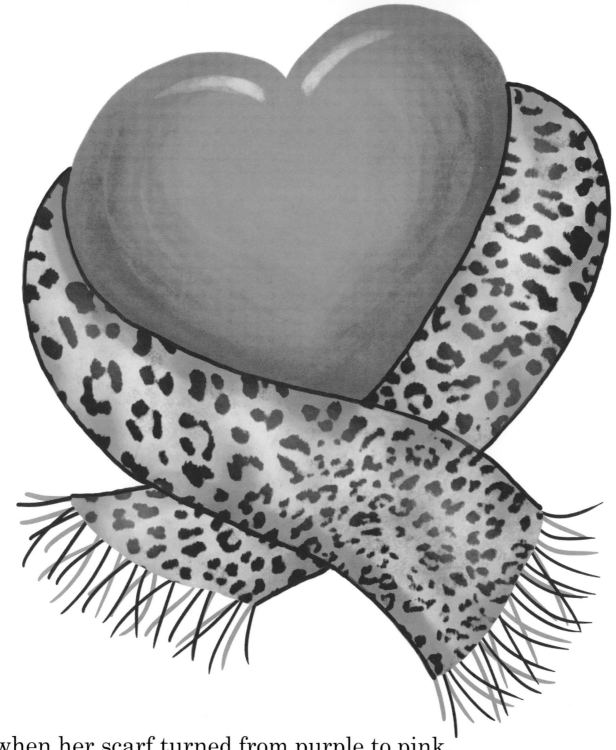

...and *that's* when her scarf turned from purple to pink.

A girl with a cape, her eyes teared up, too.
As she walked home, she knew this to be true:
That although she was little, she could always do more -
whether be kind to her family or the neighbor next door;

That what she does matters, and means a whole lot;
that it's best to be kind even when others are not.

And just as it's true with *A Girl With A Cape*,
We, too, have those powers which make us all great...

A helping hand,
a listening ear,
a loving heart,
a snack to share,
a thank you, a smile, a hug for a friend,
and once you get going, it just doesn't end.
Your kindness, like dominoes, keeps going and going
and where it ends up, there's no way of knowing!

So...

Always remember and never forget,
that what we do matters, no time for regret.
Our time here is short, and we grow up so fast...
It's when we spread kindness, our legacy lasts.

you
matter.

TIME
SEND A CARD
WALK A
FLOWERS DOG
CHEER CLEAN UP
TELL DAD YOU LOVE HIM
TIFUL I'M GLAD I KNOW YOU
WHEN YOU ARE WITH ME
FRIEND I AM BETTER FOR KNOWING YOU

So, keep your cape on and let it remind you
to do the world good and leave a trail behind you
of kind words and actions that you do and say ...

So tell me sweet reader...

got your cape on today?